Work conception: Carles Broto
Publisher: Arian Mostaedi
Graphic & Layout Design: Fernando Graells
Production & Graphic Design: Francisco Orduña
Compilation, Photo Material & Text information:
          American Book Services (USA)

Printed in Spain

transformedbuildings

INDEX

INTRODUCTION

The building is a living entity that never ceases to change throughout its existence. Reinterpreting and discovering the new possibilities of forms created with other objectives represents an intense task of imagination and creation that forces designers to handle different tools to the ones they use for designing the new.

Many questions arise when we explore old spaces and model them to create the physiognomy of a new use. It is a delicate task to achieve a balance on the fragile border between the freshness of the new language and the solemnity of the old without succumbing to nostalgia or an excessive desire to make a mark. Why then do we restore? Why not build anew and erase the past in order to write on a fresh sheet?

To restore, to preserve, to repair, to reconstruct, to intervene...this ambiguous family of terms refers to the same controversial practice that seeks to refurbish old spaces in order to give them a new use, whilst safeguarding their historical character and holding back excessive expressions of personality and genius by the designer. It is a difficult balance involving many conflicts over historical research and technical solutions, in which the architect often comes out as the loser. Why is it that we insist on altering the language of old buildings trough the use of contemporary elements?

Because restored buildings possess a permanent, provocative and fresh present time that contrasts with the dusty image that their detractors have of them. Because –with some magnificent exceptions– architecture preserved in a glass jar as a museum piece reconstructed stone by stone, tends to be sterile architecture. When all is said and done, architecture is the paradigm of useful art, and as such it is forced to be continually rejuvenated in order to shelter the users that over the years inhabit it, sleep, eat and work in it, or simply walk through it.

Vicen Cornu & Benoit Crépet

Photographs: Jean Marie Mothiers & Benoit Crépet

Le Musée du Théatre Forain

ArtenayFrance

After the municipality of the French village of Artenay inherited some years ago the stage property of a troupe of itinerant players, it was decided to create a museum of ambulant theatre as the centrepiece of a whole area's renovation. Apart from the museum, the programme was rounded out by a local archaeological exhibition, reserves and work-shops for the museum of ambulant theatre, plus a documentation centre and a small public library. The only new constructions are a small theatre, reception and administrative spaces, temporary exhibition spaces and a dwelling adjoining the museum.

The architects saw this set of ordinary rural buildings as a landscape, federating their diversity into a coherent whole and restoring an old itinerary around a new communal facility.

In order to conserve the balance of the place while asserting its new vocation, the architects magnified the walls which they saw as vital to its identity, and manifested the presence of the new interior facilities by way of the openings.

Windows and doors were redistributed on the existing facades, restored with a careful eye for traditional stonework details. Woodwork and doorways were treated as noble elements and built by local craftsmen. The new wing, designed to close the yard of the Paradis farm that backs onto the mall, shows the same concern for unity and dialogue with neighbouring forms. Permanent exhibition rooms are housed in what was once the main barn of the farm, the structure of which was laid bare and the render renewed. Linked by ramps and a footbridge, they compose a complex itinerary distributed over two levels on either side of the full-height central volume that structures the whole.

Materials suggest refined rustic taste: terra cotta floors, solid woodwork, and render painted white to distinguish restored walls from partitions. The original door was enlarged and rebuilt with particular care. When it is open wide, the central volume is opened to nearly six metres, transforming the space into a stage for spectators gathered in the courtyard.

9

Site plan

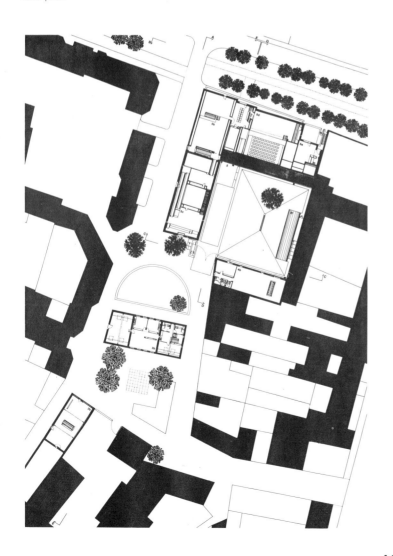

The program consists of the rehabilitation of a set of buildings of agricultural origin. The vocabulary, based on the dialogue between white cloth and woodwork, seeks to unify the buildings.

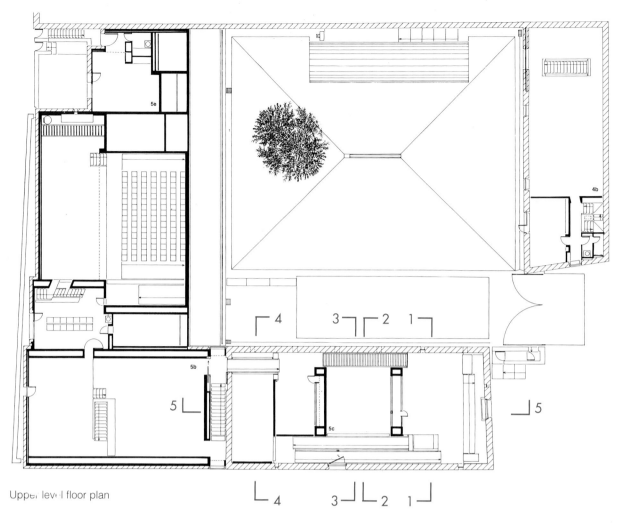

Upper level floor plan

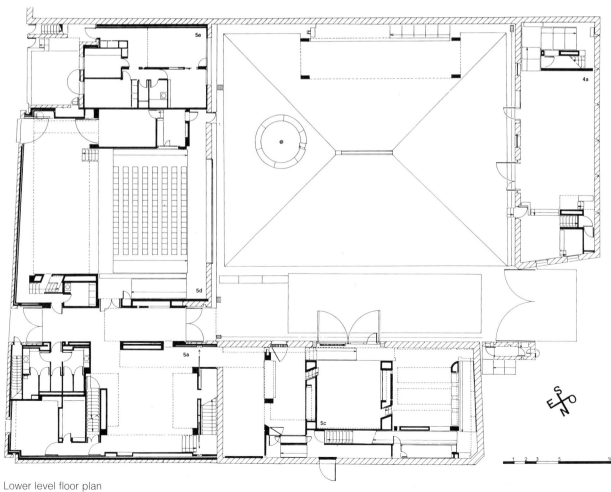

Lower level floor plan

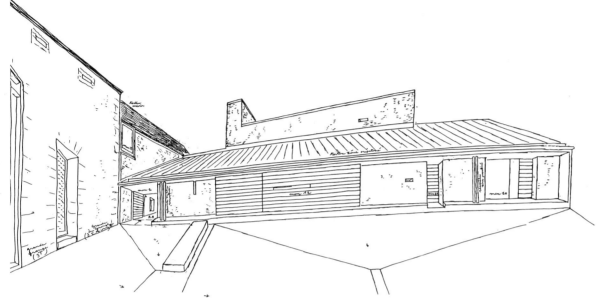
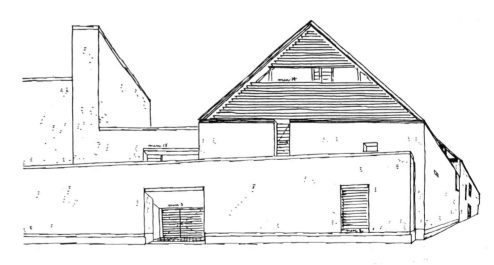

13

Perspectives of the exhibition spaces

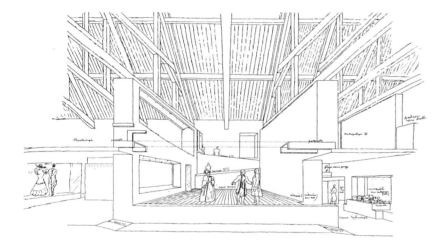

The museum spaces were organised in an orderly tour in accordance with the rhythm of life of a theatrical company at various times in history. The assembly shows elements referring to the arrival of the actors at a village, various aspects of the performance and their departure.

5-5

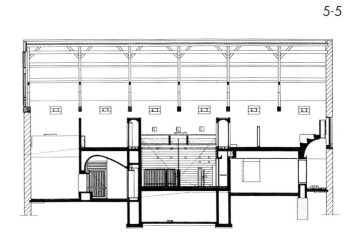

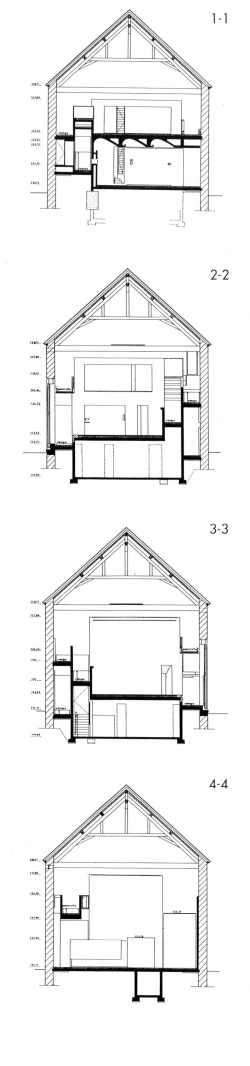

1-1

2-2

3-3

4-4

The central room of the museum is covered by a sculptural truss that has been preserved and restored, as can be seen in the photograph above the caption

16

The architectural vocabulary of the rehabilitation is attentive to the character of the place and to a knowledge of the local architecture.

Josep Llinàs

Photographs: Lourdes Jansana

TarragonaSpain

Built in 1908 and owned by the Tarragona Bishopric, the *Teatre del Patronat Obrer* was one of the first commissions that the catalan modernist architect Josep Maria Jujol received as an independent architect. Like many others, it was a very modest remodeling job for small theatrical representations, year-end school promenades, and local ceremonies held by organizations associated to the church. But discord between Jujol and the ownership which still remains a mystery prevented him from finishing his work. During the Spanish Civil War, air raids caused major damages in the foyer. Years later, inconsiderate remodeling work done to block out sources of natural light, to install restrooms and to comply with safety codes marred the theater in its metamorphosis into the Metropol Movie House.

In the 80s, the building was left abandoned, and the Metropol suffered from accelerated decay. Finally, a few years ago, the Tarragona City Hall purchased the Metropol to turn it into municipal theatre. The rehabilitation program was commissioned to the architect Josep Llinàs, specialized in the work of Jujol. The work received the FAD Architectural Prize in 1996.

The refurbishing work turned out to be complex, full of hesitation and highly diversified, mostly due to the lack of documentation on the original building. Like many other projects of Jujol's, the theater was built on an extremely tight budget using strictly local materials. They knew from the architect's son himself, that he had conceived it as a representation of a religious allegory, a boat, where the theatergoers embark and are saved amidst life's tempestous waters. When analyzing the design, Llinàs realized that the idea of a boat had guided the transformation of the building components, making them part of a whole. He also reached the conclusion that the theoretical water level was just at the level of the foyer floor, below which everything would be submerged.

Starting out with this, the Llinàs team made new additions in the dressing rooms and the stagehouse, remodeled areas such as the entrance hall that Jujol had never worked on, and orthodox rebuilding on the part of the foyer that had fallen in the air raid as well as on work that had disfigured Jujol's architecture leaving various remains. In addition, some parts of the building that Jujol himself was probably unable to finish, were concluded.

In the top picture, perspective view of the entrance leading in from the rambla de Tarragona. All elements from earlier inappropriate restoration work were removed.

Longitudinal section

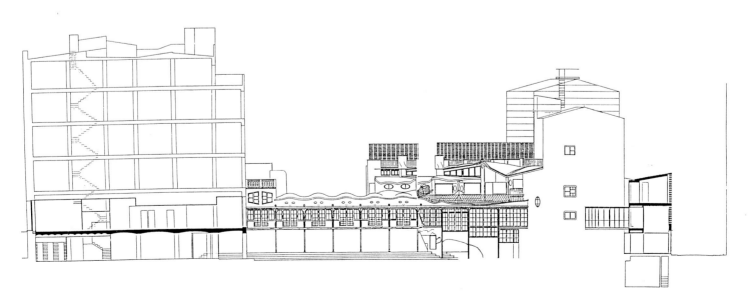

Plan of the teathre at second balcony level

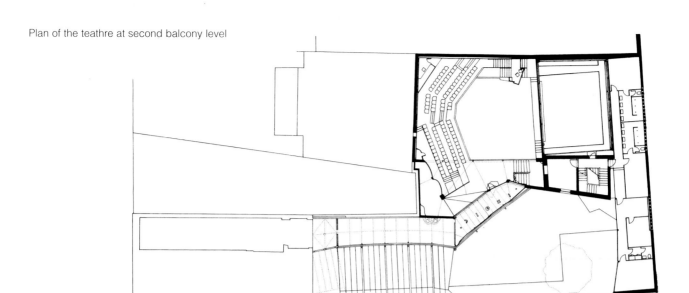

Plan of the teathre at level of the first balcony

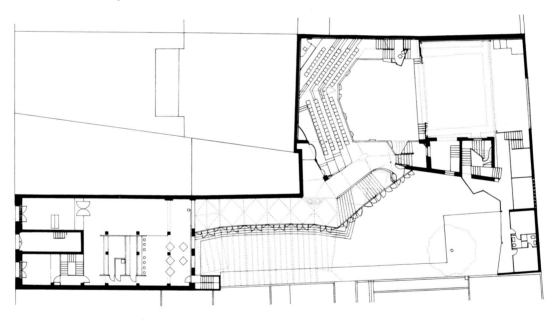

Plan of the teathre at orchestra level

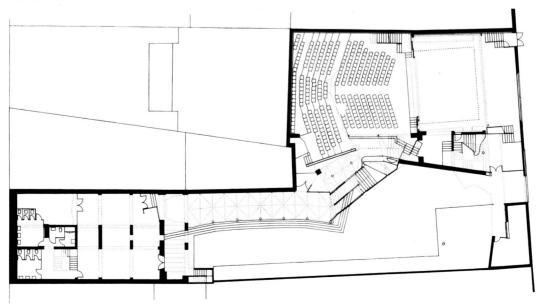

In the reconstruction process of the Theater Metropol, it was considered essential to preserve and restore all Jujol's original elements such as the flooring, railings, engravings and paintings.

Josep Llinás project seeks to meet the
needs of a present-day theater efficiently
and at the same time to strike up a respectful dialogue with this magnificent example of
modernista architecture.

Cross section

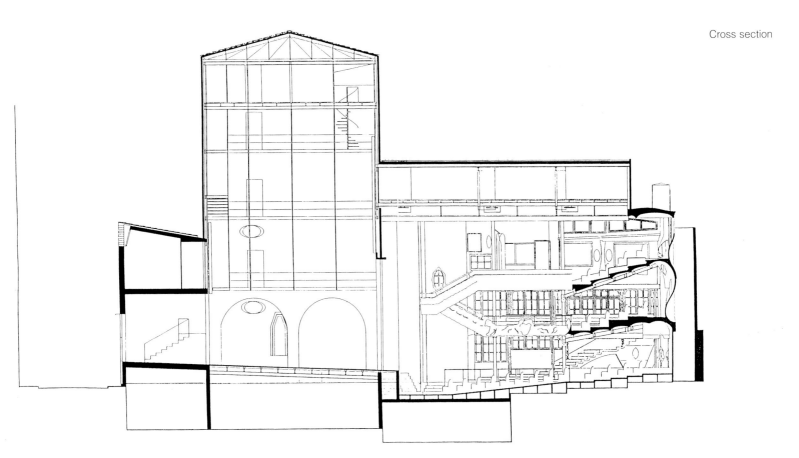

27

Claudio
Lazzarini & Carl
Pickering

Residence on Sicilian Coast

Sicily Italy

In this conversion of a 19th-century seaside villa in south-eastern Sicily into a contemporary holiday home, the client wanted a new interior –a landing with three rooms, two bathrooms and stairs overlooking a sitting room– in an existing space with double-height ceiling. The intense Sicilian light glancing off local stone immediately imposed itself as a central theme. The villa's roof was opened to bring light into all the floors through skylights that are screened by external blinds in summer. To mark out the new windows on the elevations –loopholes landward, large ports seaward– the stone of the walls was *dematerialised* by a 30° chamfer.

Inside, the staircase is a scroll of blackened steel set in a cylindrical volume that forms a well of light, the pivot of a natural air-conditioning system that refers to Arab and Norman vernacular.

An eight-centimetre slit in the central wall of the living room runs up eight metres to the terrace. It is toplit and throws a tracer blade of light into the room during the day, which varies its swath according to the seasons like a sundial.

Like an ode to Mediterranean light and the sea wind, this project –which was two years in the making– is a manifesto: the elegance of its honed spaces is rounded out by elaborate yet discreet details. The villa is a concentrate of the architects' love for the stone of the South and the refined use of *poor* traditional materials. It bears witness to their skill in inventing or reinterpreting highly functional construction systems in an artistic way.

Photographs: Giovanna Cipparrone

The new openings on the exterior of the villa take the form of small narrow cracks. They are thus distinguished and are super-imposed clearly on the existing openings without altering the general image of the building.

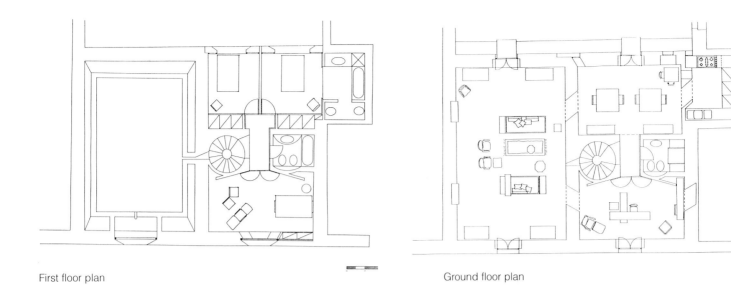

First floor plan

Ground floor plan

The elegance and sobriety of the interior spaces, in which the use of traditional materials prevails, is compensated by small details that are elaborate and discreet. On this page, images of the crack in the central wall of the living room.

A/A Cross section

B/B Cross section

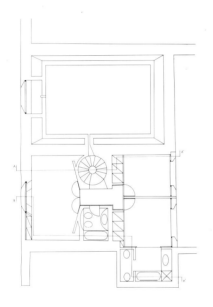

The dematerialisation of the bevelled angles, the unexpected cuts in the walls, the skylights and the angled openings create unexpected perspectives of the interior of the dwelling and allow a greater connection between rooms with minimum modifications to the original structure.

An organic spiral staircase communicates the ground floor with the upper level and the terrace, which is protected by a light glass and metal structure.

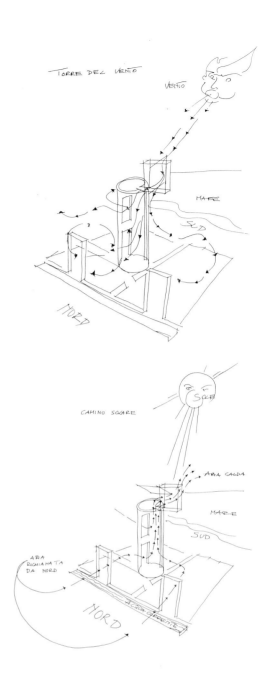

Ottorino Berselli
Cecilia Cassina

Residenza *in*
Puegnago del Garda

Photographs: Alberto Piovano

MonteAcutoItaly

In the Italian hills of Valtenesi, overlooking Lake Garda, stands the small town of Monte Acuto. It is presided over by a tower with an old dovecot, a construction typical of the plain of Padania but uncommon in this region.

The restoration project covered one corner of the old town, which dates back to the end of the sixth century and is dominated by the massive quadrangular tower. The whole complex was in an advanced state of disrepair, particularly the tower, and a thorough restoration was therefore carried out on several levels.

The project was based on the idea of retrieving previously existing elements, with particular attention to interpreting everything that, through the successive layers that had been superimposed over the years, bore clear indications of its past. The project therefore proposed a reassessment of the whole town, despite the fact that it directly affected only a fragment of it, "in an attempt to regain lost urban emotions," in the words of the authors in their report on the project.

The theme running through the new work is light, which assumes the main role in the scheme as a result of the generous, yet subtle, openings. The serene atmosphere of the interior of the old tower (now converted into a dwelling) is bathed in light entering through clean slits running the length of the ceiling on the first two floors, where the main rooms are situated.

The materials used –palette-applied intonaco on the walls, and coloured cement and natural oak on the floors– endow all the rooms with a homogeneous feel. The distribution of the rooms was problematic due to the unusual structure of the house, particularly the top storey, formerly used as a dovecot. The solution finally adopted was to have the ground floor as the day area (living room, kitchen, bathroom, etc.) and the first floor as the night area (bedrooms). The remaining floors (the second and third floors and the former dovecot) contain the guest rooms, various study areas and a library, with panoramic views over the lake.

South elevation

The project involved the restoration and renovation of an old building featured by a tower crowned with a dovecot.
Now converted into a dewlling, before the reparation the complex offered an advance state of disrepair.

North elevation

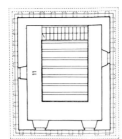

Third floor plan and dovecot

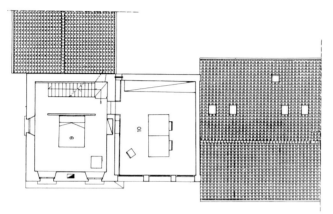

Second floor plan

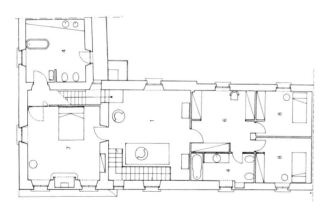

First floor plan

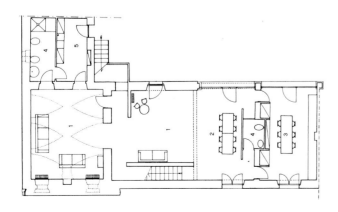

Ground floor plan

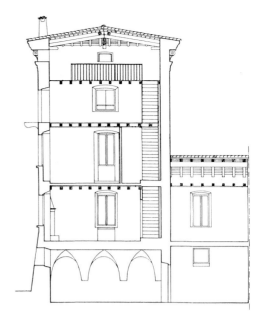

Section A-A

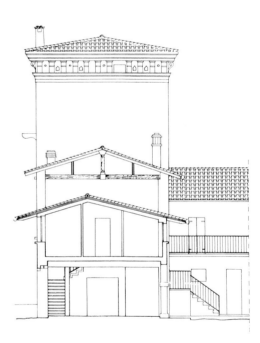

Section B-B

The homogenous finish given to the interiors enables the project to be interpreted as a whole.

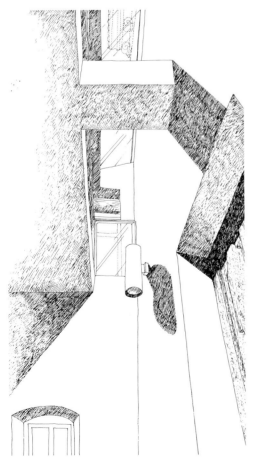

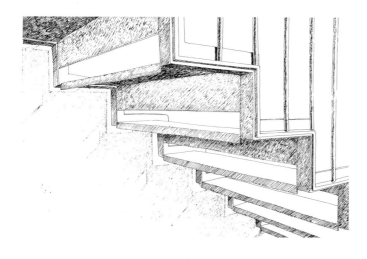

Broad transversal openings run the length of the roof, providing the main on the first two floors with generous but subtle lighting. The study and library occupy the old dovecot.

Francesco Delogu Gaetano Lixi

Photographs: Roberto Bossaglia

Castello Catrani

Umbria Italy

Restoration of the Castello di Petriolo in a valley not far from Cittá di Castello, in the Italian district of Umbria, has resulted in refurbished interiors, fully adapted to modern living requirements, combined with total respect for the historical fabric of the building itself.

Built in medieval times as part of the nearby town's defensive network, the castle complex has numerous architectural stratifications testifying to the variety of uses it has been put to over the centuries, from noble residence to farming state house.

In 1736, Marco Antonio Catrani, counsellor of the Roman Curia, redesigned the main façade, making two large bulwarks to acces the courtyard, and some interior modifications.

The recent project by Delogu and Lixi focuses the conversion of the complex into a set of private dwellings. So they made a general conservative restoration plan and organized its division into four separate apartments.

The so-called *chapel apartment* featured here occupies only part of the wing on the left of the main portal. Its three-level design incorporates the previous layout without overwhelming it, creating beautifully contrived contrasts between austerity and complexity.

The project was initiated in 1993, work was begun in 1994, and today the rest of the residential units are still under construction.

General floor plan

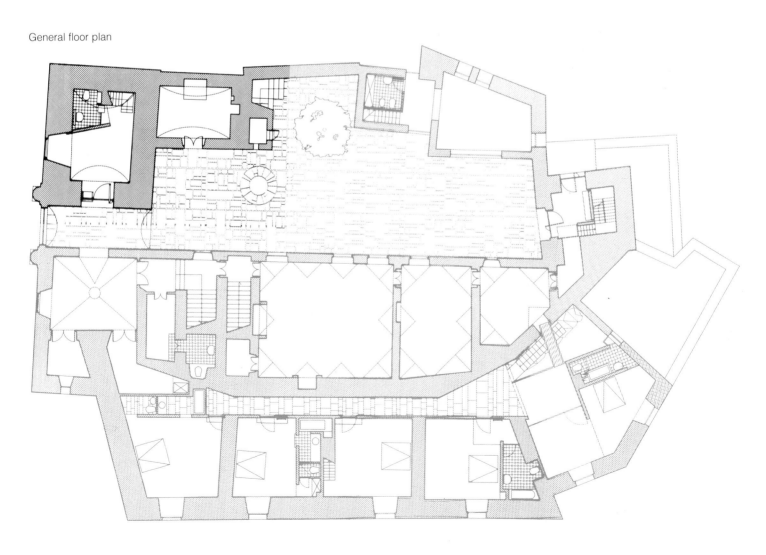

The entrance courtyard of the castle, the restoration of which was limited to conserving existing elements. The courtyard is flanked by the chapel apartment, so called because the interior incorporates the former chapel of the castle.

On this double page, several views of the iron walkway. It leads through the opening made in the thick supporting wall that separates it from the chapel and into the kitchen.

The botton picture shows the ground floor bathroom. All the moving partitions and built-in furish-ings in the apartment are in oak wood.

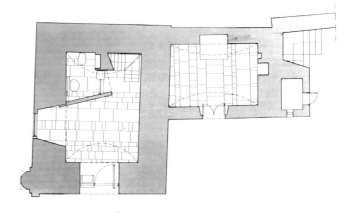

Ground floor plan

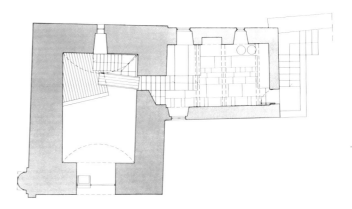

First floor plan

Second floor plan

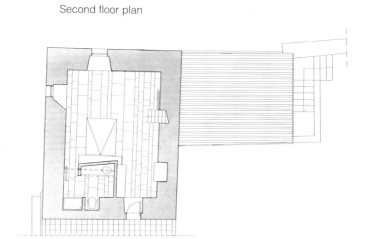

On this page, views of the kitchen, located just above the original site of the chapel of the castle.

The courtyord leads directly into the living room trough a door built in steel and glass which incorporates an oak seat the inside. In the background, the staircase leads to the upper floors.

Longitudinal Section

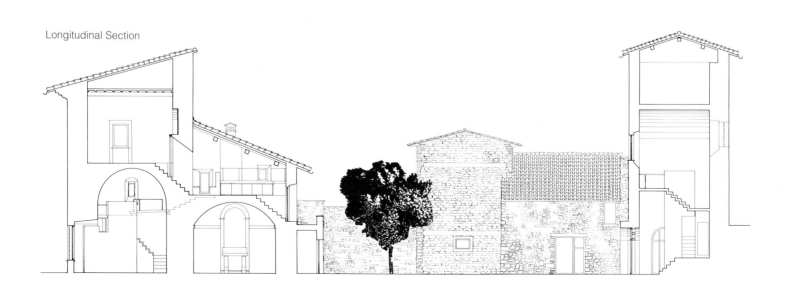

Enric Miralles
Benedetta Tagliabue

Photographs: Eugeni Pons

Loft in Barcelona

BarcelonaSpain

The architects have restored an abandoned building of the historical centre of Barcelona, in which the walls had been demolished and the sequence of the old rooms was only read through the different types of flooring.

The fundamental decision was to leave the space as they found it –a single nave developed around the central courtyard– and to reconstruct the floors, re-installing the original tiles according to a different plan. Instead of following the perimeter of the old walls, they were arranged according to the patches of light coming in through the windows.

The dividing walls were conceived as curtains forming a room, but without interrupting the free circular passage. The idea of the curtains also later turned into a series of mobile wooden elements such as tables and doors. That, together with the floors, represents the most designed part of the house. In this sense, the most important element is Unstable Table, which is thoroughly mobile and is almost a small house in itself.

The rest of the work was generated by the house itself, and the architects accepted what it offered in the course of the construction: large fragments of Gothic arches, 18th-century paintings, false marble, handmade tiles discovered behind walls and coarse rough render revealed a succession of residences stratified one over the other from the Middle Ages to the Modernista period.

In the main living space, both the Gothic arches and subsequent filling work have been left exposed. The new intervention focused on two main elements: a labyrinthine bookshelf built with a simple system of welded irons that turns around the walls; and two walls that clarify the perspective and give the rectangular living area the form of a bottleneck.

The main bedroom and bathroom occupy one of the previous rooms with views of the garden. In the new bedroom the architects used doors and windows from an old house that was being demolished in another part of the city.

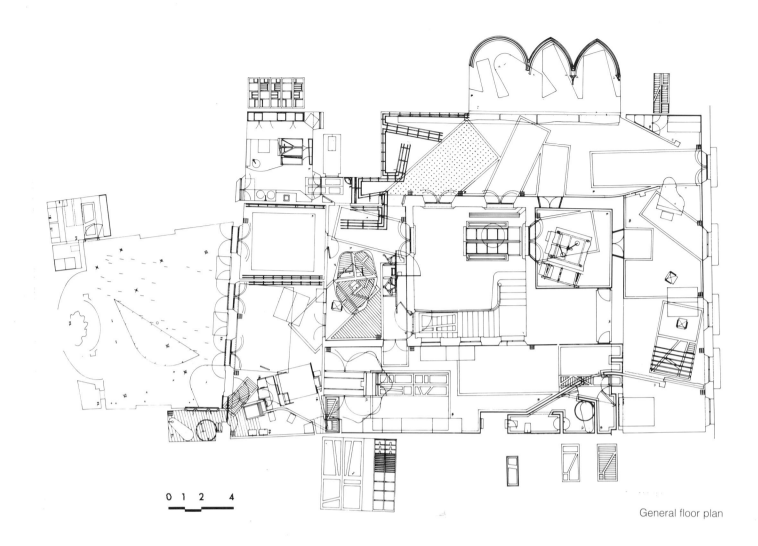

General floor plan

The stripping of the walls revealed gothic arches with capitals and 18th-century paintings, which have been conserved and converted into elements that characterise each room.

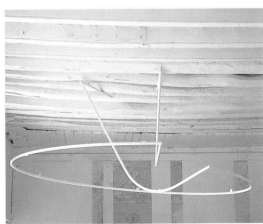

Two views of the main living room. The walls that form the rooms have been conceived as dividing curtains that at no time interrupt the circular passage.

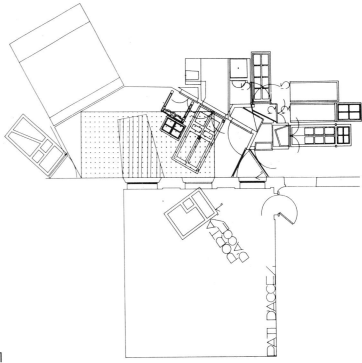

At the top of the previous page, a view of the "Unstable Table". It is a completely mobile element that can adapt to infinite positions and functions as a small house in itself.

The main room is organised around
several mobile oak partitions.

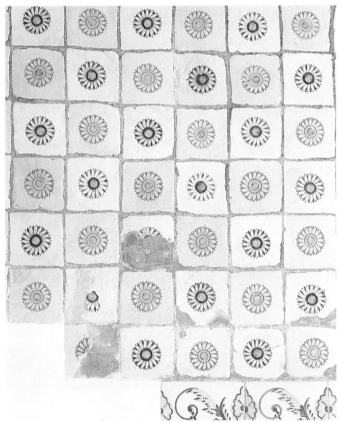

The existing flooring has been rebuilt and placed according to another scheme. In some parts the new arrangement is inspired –according to the architects– by the patches of light coming through the windows.

Susanna Lumsden
Dillon Patrick

Photographs: Philip Bier / View

House in Holland **Park**

London United Kingdom

The project is an unusual modern house that has been carved out of the structure of an existing Church Hall. The client required a modern home with one large living space on a single floor. Few residential buildings lend themselves to this kind of conversion and most commercial buildings considered were either too large or had low ceilings.

The derelict Church Hall struck the right balance among all the requirements. Its core was a 20 x 8 metre hall, built in the late 19th century with a smaller hall to one side and raised stage at one end. Both rooms were well lit form above by dormer windows and lanterns. The aim was to insert a completely new set of living spaces into the shell of the main hall, stage and smaller hall.

By demolishing outbuildings at the back, the structure was reduced to its simplest elements and opened up to the garden. A clear distinction was drawn between the old core and the new additions. The shell was refurbished using traditional materials while the design of the new insertions (a staircase, two partitions and a mezzanine floor) emphasise their distinctness and modernity and uses materials from a carefully graded palette: glass mosaic, unpainted render and lacquered steel.

The result is powerful tension between modern elements and the traditional building that houses them. The design visibly acknowledges the building's former institutional character and structure but adds a series of new layers which have transformed it from an obsolete shell into a spacious and unusual home.

With the demolition of the secondary buildings
behind the rear facade, the structure was reduced
to in basic elements, and the living space was
completely opened up to the garden at the rear.

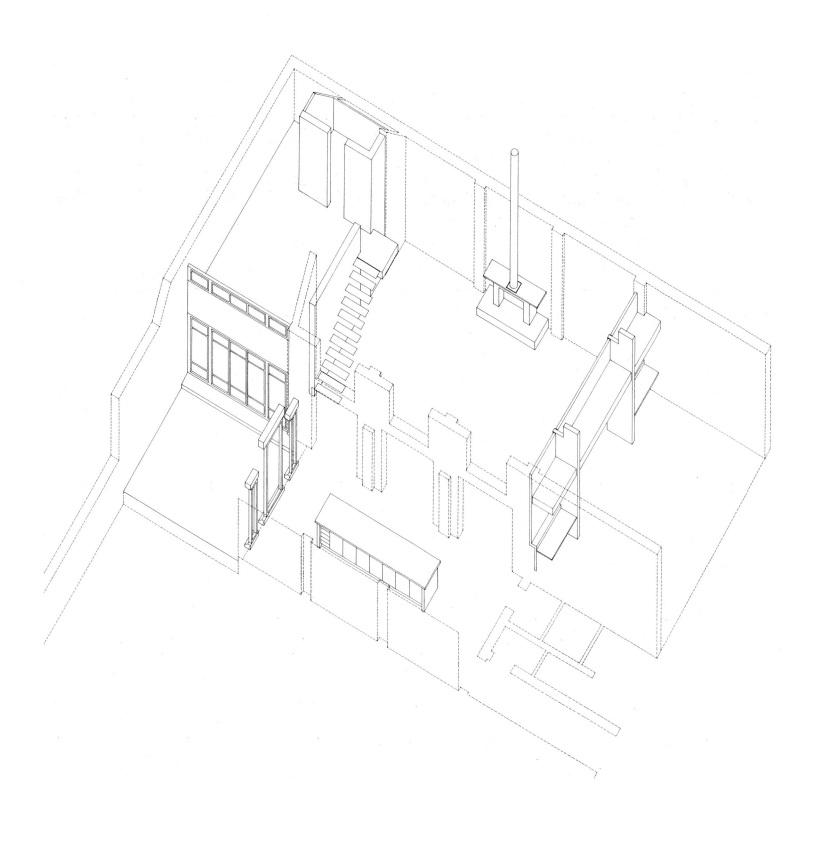

The core of the house is formed by a hall 60 feet high, built at the end of the nineteenth century. The space is bathed in generous zenithal light entering trough skylights inserted in the roof.

Ground floor plan and penthouse

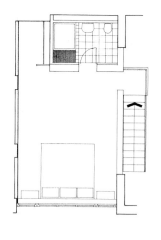

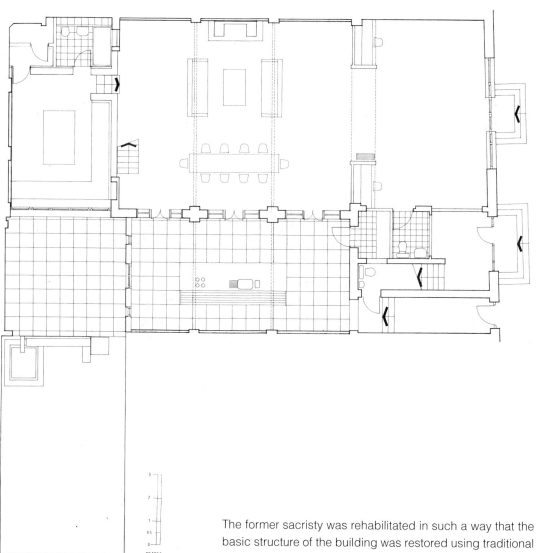

The former sacristy was rehabilitated in such a way that the basic structure of the building was restored using traditional systems, whereas the new construction elements clearly state their modernity.

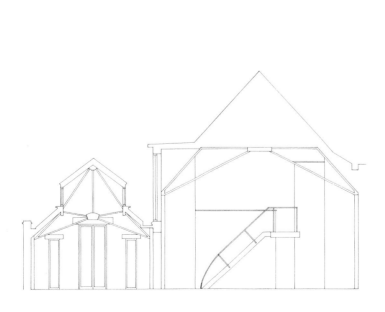

Cross section

73

Fausto Colombo

Palazzo Cavagna-Sangiuliani

Photographs: Cesare Colombo

PaviaItaly

With its F-shaped plan, Palazzo Cavagna-Sangiu-liani in the centre of old Pavia is an interesting example of late Quattrocento Pavian architecture - renaissance architectural design had to be adapted to the spatial constraints of a medieval urban fabric - that also testifies to the stylistic changes of later centuries. Skilful restoration of the almost derelict palazzo to convert it into a home and a notary's office has removed these later additions to reveal the hidden symmetries, rhythmical scansion and frescoes of the original structure. The decomposition and subsequent re-composition of the various parts has made the palazzo a multi-purpose building once again. The restored building is laid out around three courtyards on three floors, each serving a particular function.

The ground floor is devoted entirely to offices. With direct access from the street, the large vaulted hall houses the reception and secretarial office. The hall divides the meeting room from the notary's private office and is the hub of the office complex. The meeting room has walls decorated with renaissance frescoes of the Lombardy school (the maidens and hunting scenes are unusual in Pavia), a coffered ceiling and an oak and walnut floor bordered with stone. A camber-arched wall with glass in the upper part and sliding leaf doors below separates the meeting room from the waiting area.

The first floor is the day area of perspectively sequenced rooms placed along the internal facade. The wooden ceiling and the stone floor are linked by their geometric design.

The second floor houses the spaces for study and rest. What it loses in distributive clarity, it gains in composition and in the variety of unusual elements. The homogeneity of the treatment of walls and floors and the diffuse luminosity tend to provide visual uniformity. This conversion aims to recover the image of the residential palazzo structured around a courtyard and open to the city, thus contributing to the reorganisation of the old centre and the requalification of the environmental context.

The building is organised spatially through two inner court-yards separated from the body of the building through a third courtyard. These can be accessed directly from the street.

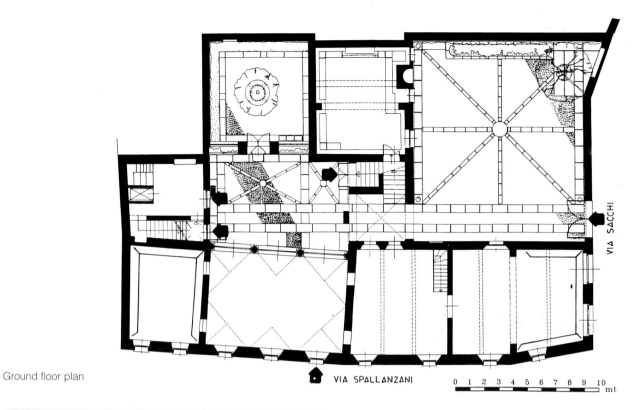

Ground floor plan

VIA SPALLANZANI

VIA SACCHI

0 1 2 3 4 5 6 7 8 9 10 mt

In the second inner courtyard the pavement has been restored. It is built of river pebbles in the Lombardy style, following a geometric plan traced in stone.

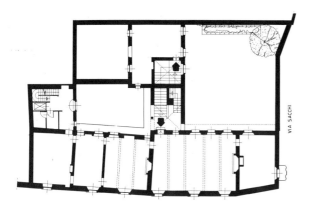

First floor plan

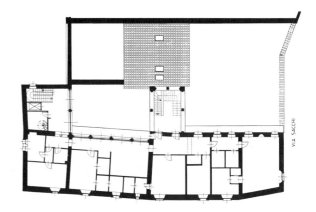

Second floor plan

The upper floor opens onto the inner courtyard through a loggia supported by free-standing stone columns crowned by small capitals. This loggia runs along the whole length of one of the outer walls of the second courtyard.

Longitudinal section

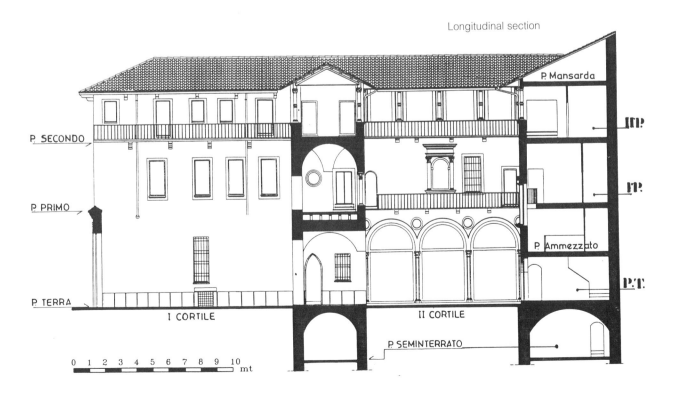

P. SECONDO

P. PRIMO

P. TERRA

I CORTILE

II CORTILE

P. SEMINTERRATO

P. Mansarda

II P.

I P.

P. Ammezzato

P.T.

0 1 2 3 4 5 6 7 8 9 10 mt

81

Roberto Menghi

Photographs: Melina Mulas

Castello nel Lodigiano

LodigianoItaly

The aim of the project was to restore the north-western part of the Castle, modernizing the interior and making it fully inhabitable, without spoiling the unique character it had taken on over the years.

New connections have been made between the ground and the first floors through two new spiral steel staircases with steps in solid bay oak; the existing straight staircase in stone was resurfaced. The horizontal structures on the first floor, original beams and shelves in bay oak, were restored and reinforced with a special procedure based on resins and metal inserts.The existing terracota tile floors were levelled off and integrated with new hand made tiles of the same size made with the same clay (which is still found in the area) as the old ones. To solve the problem of rising damp, which has, for centuries, been penetrating the wall an insulation system using "active electro-osmosis" has been adopted with excellent results. On the other hand, the project creates an intermediate level between the ground and the first floor, in part adapted as a study-library facing over the main hall, in part used as a service area: cloakroom, laundry, etc. The six meter ceiling height typ-ical of the age has been maintained for entrance hall, part of the main hall and the whole kitchen. The intermediate level has been made, like the stairs, using steel structures, but with a load-bearing flooring in Swedish pine. The two stairways and this last space were designed and constructed with materials that constrast with the original context, in order to highlight their superestructural and "removable" nature. Bedrooms, bathrooms and closets have been fitted into the space situated above the pointed arches, which was once a hay loft. The outer wall of the bedrooms, overlooking the courtyard has been moved back with respect to the rest of the façade, in order to make room for a long balcony, about two meters wide, above the arches.

The Castle looks like a fortress with a moat, having surrounding walls and a shortage of apertures, with a consequent shortage of light and air in the rooms. This problem was solved by reopening some of the original apertures that had been walled over and making some new horizontal slits under the western eaves.

The roof has been restored and insulated, maintaining the existing cover in hand-made bent tiles.

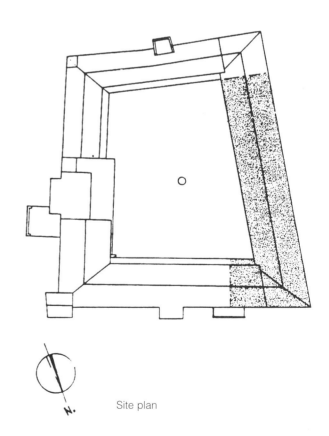

Site plan

The project consists of the restoration of the north-west part of the castle by transforming the interior into a modern residence without modifying the original character of the historical building, which appears from the outside as a walled fort with few openings.

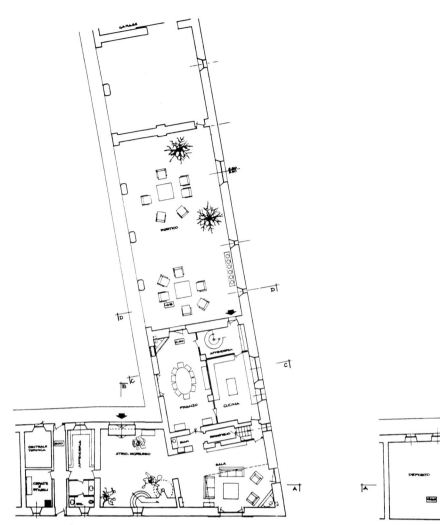

Ground floor plan

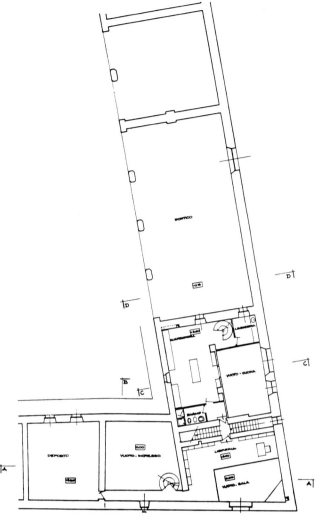

Intermediate level

On the right-hand page, views of the large courtyard of the castle, with large porticoes providing spaces protected from direct sunlight.

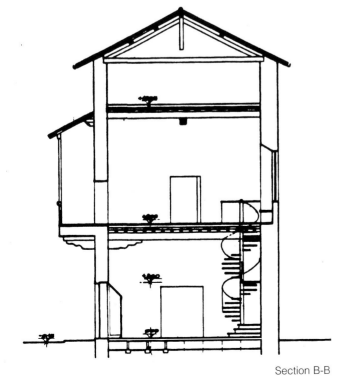

Section B-B

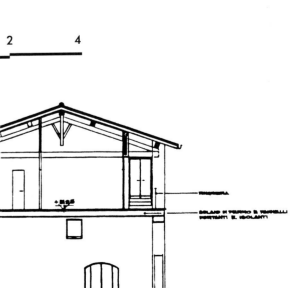

Section D-D

Part of the intervention consisted in insert-ing a new level between the ground floor (6 meters high) and the upper level, and establishing a new vertical connection by means of a new spiral staircase with solid oak steps.

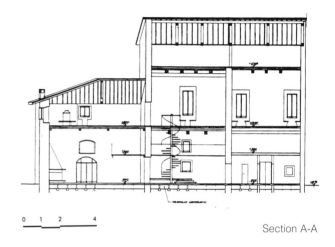

0 1 2   4

Section A-A

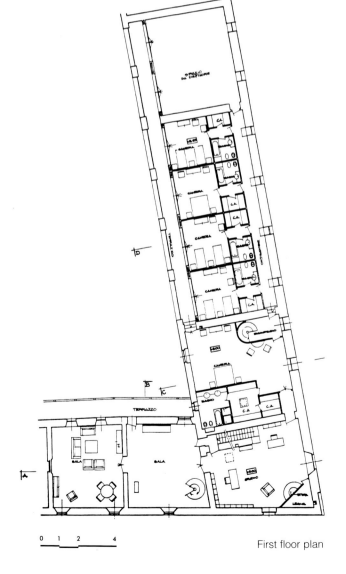

First floor plan

The original loadbearing structure made of wooden trusses has been treated with resins for conservation and reinforced with metal elements.

Beat Consoni

Photographs: Markus Baumgartner

The Gnädinger house

St. GallenSuiza

The Gnädinger house was built at the end of the last century. It is located in a forest near the city of St. Gallen. The building was in poor condition, so the facades needed restoration and there was a need for a new kitchen, a bathroom and central heating, as well as a new garage-workshop. The interior rooms were altered to meet current standards and requirements, without making changes to the structure and static construction means of the old house.

The new technical facilities, such as the kitchen and the bathroom, are concentrated in a compact unit, which takes up a separate section horizontally and vertically within the frame of the old stable. The structures of this cube are kept separate from the

house's original statics. The floor plan of the garage-workshop is a square.

This small building sets up a new relation between the ensemble and its surroundings.

The construction is made of concrete, steel and glass.

The main goal of the renovation of the old house was to reproduce construction techniques of yesterday using the materials and knowledge of today. The stable unit was originally built of large wooden boards, which were replaced with large bakelite-treated wooden boards. The original facade covering, consisting of wooden shingles, was renewed with horizontal wood strips. The west facade, traditionally closed as a protection against wind and rain, and originally covered with several layers of wood-shingles, was given a new covering of translucent polycarbonate panels, allowing natural light to enter the building but at the same time not spoiling the character of this closed wall. With one true window and the original wood-clad wall underneath painted blue, the facade takes on a certain complexity, despite remaining a single unit.

Site plan

The construction of a new pavilion made it possible to establish a new type of relationship between the old building and the context in which it is located.

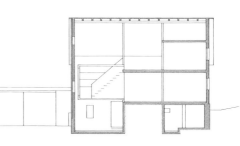

Cross section

The new pavilion, used as a garage and workshop, was built using only exposed concrete, steel and glass.

First floor plan

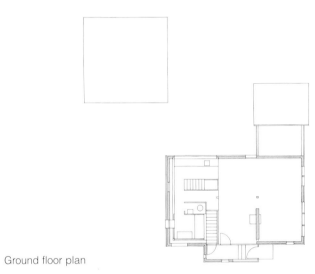

Ground floor plan

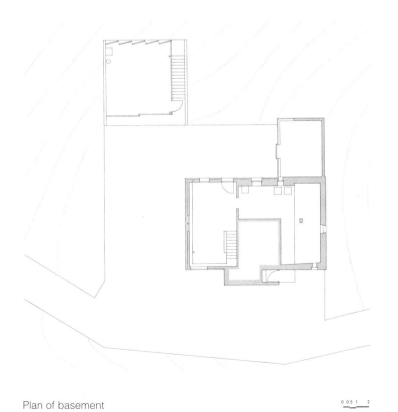

Plan of basement

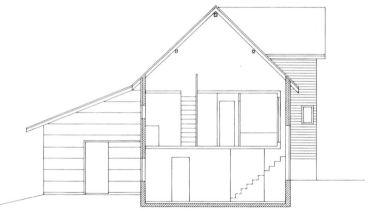

Cross section

The west facade was clad with translucent polycarbonate panels to maintain the idea of a closed facade without preventing the entrance of natural light.

Adolf Krischanitz

Kunshalle Krems

Photographs: Gerald Zugmann

KremsAustria

The new art gallery occupies a side and the interior of an abandoned tobacco factory. On the ground floor, roughly rendered and steeply sloping columns beneath short-span vaults constrained the space. Above this, two rows of columns, some of wood, some of cast iron, create three aisles through two production shops.

Krischanitz's scheme treated the structure of the existing building with great care. The new concrete stele in front of the entrance is the only visible indication that anything has changed inside the building. The yellow of the walls and the brown of the windows relate to the world of tobacco. The careful juxtaposition of old and new is also seen in the fact that the drainpipes of the all new parts of the building are under the eaves of the old building.

Krischanitz places a large up-ended cuboid in the courtyard, a new stone element which creates a space through its relationship to the old building. It has a mezzanine with an exhibition hall that has perfect environmental control and is lit from the sides by high-level windows which can be blacked out. Under this is a stepped lecture theatre. A two-storey service corridor on one side and a set of ramps on the other provide connections to the old building. Together they surround the courtyard which is now smaller than before and has a glazed roof forming a top-lit atrium.

The colour scheme of the new parts of the building is based on the grey of the exposed concrete. The spatial density of the entrance hall contrasts strikingly with the spaciousness of the large atrium with its glass roof.

From the ramps visitors can look through a row of slender columns into the hall, and then as they climb higher they can look down onto it.

The new art gallery is located in an old tobacco factory. Except for the new concrete stela located at the entrance, nothing seems to   indicate the change that has been made in the interior.

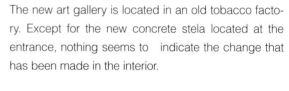

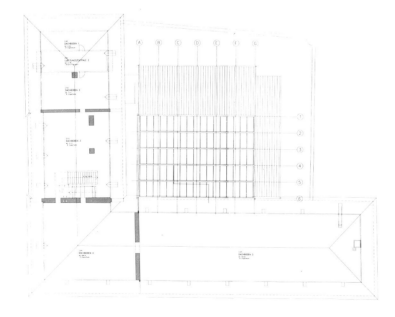

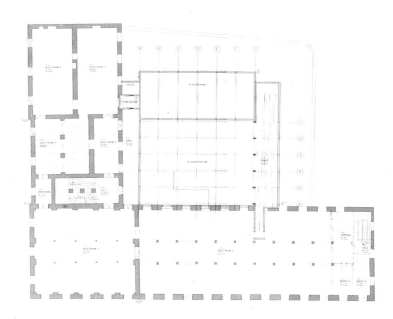

First floor plan

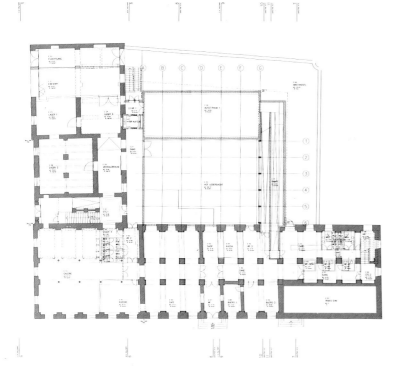

Ground floor plan

Basement floor plan

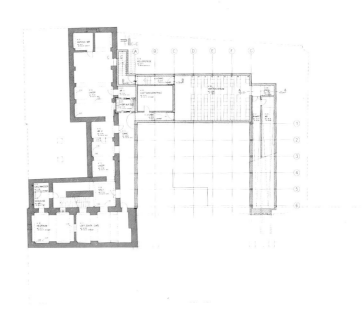

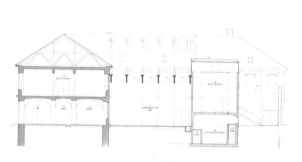

Section 8-8

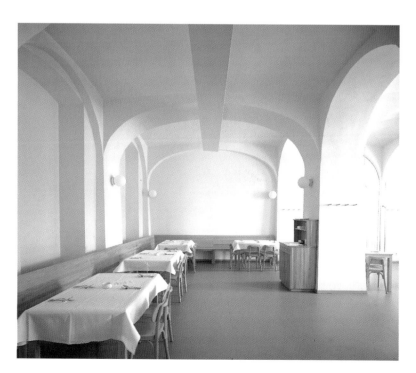

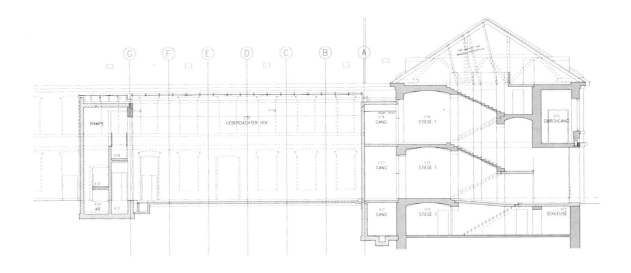

Guillermo Vázquez Consuegra

Photographs: Duccio Malagamba

Instituto Andaluz del Patrimonio Histórico

Sevilla Spain

La Cartuja de Santa María de las Cuevas can be regarded as a miniature city standing opposite Seville and also fenced in by it, on the banks of the River Guadalquivir. Like any urban entity, it has undergone a continuous process of modification over its five centuries of existence. A dense network of kilns, chimneys, bell towers and spires rises over the island as a witness to its chequered history. Originally, in the fifteenth century, it was a Carthusian monastery, only to become a famous pottery in the first half of the nineteenth century under the management of the English entrepreneur Pickman. The complex became increasingly chaotic and labyrinthine, the more recent industrial structures blending in with and superimposing themselves on the earlier religious buildings to create a unique pattern of relationships between the two.

This was the situation when part of the complex was given a thorough restoration for the Universal Exposition of 1992, which was held on the island. Three years later, another section was inaugurated to house the offices and workshops of the Heritage Institute of the Department of Culture of the Andalusian government, leaving a further section of the complex still to be restored.

The project for this last stage, by the architect Guillermo Vázquez Consuegra, focuses on the so-called Manufacturing Area, characterized by industrial installations and featuring few religious elements. The scheme works from the basis of considering the sector as a conglomeration of parts. It emphasizes its episodic, discontinuous nature and attempts to construct its edges appropriately, add new buildings and complete fragments, at the same time respecting the unique urban quality of the original building with its cloisters, alleys and catwalks.

The first stages of the construction work were carried out without a programme of uses, so that the remains of the old buildings would suggest the route to take. In this way, a new architecture was proposed that sought its origins in the experience of that which already existed. However, the architect stressed the importance of not overestimating the remains for the mere fact of their antiquity, but for their architectural, constructional and historical value. Some elements were therefore demolished, only those considered to be of quality being preserved. The intention was to create an architecture free of formal and stylistic mimicry, capable of inserting itself naturally into the long process of growth and transformation of this group of monumental buildings.

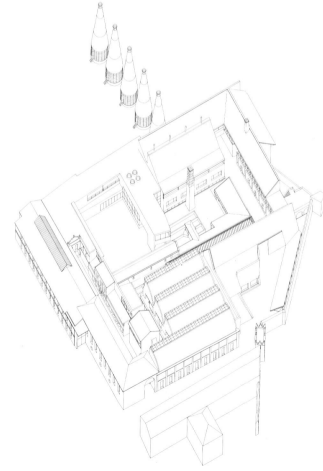

As can be seen in the picture on the right, the interior of the complex is reached throught a large archway. Only high-quality existing architectural features were preserved, and those lacking any value were removed.

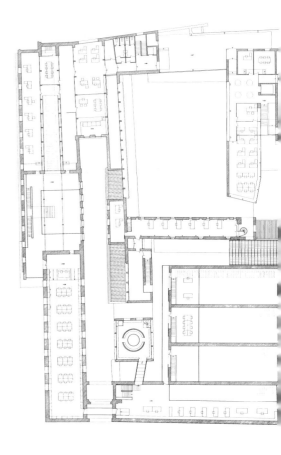

On this double page: views of the historical complex from the outside and from the interior courtyards around which it is organized.

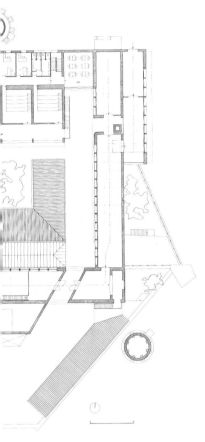

First floor plan

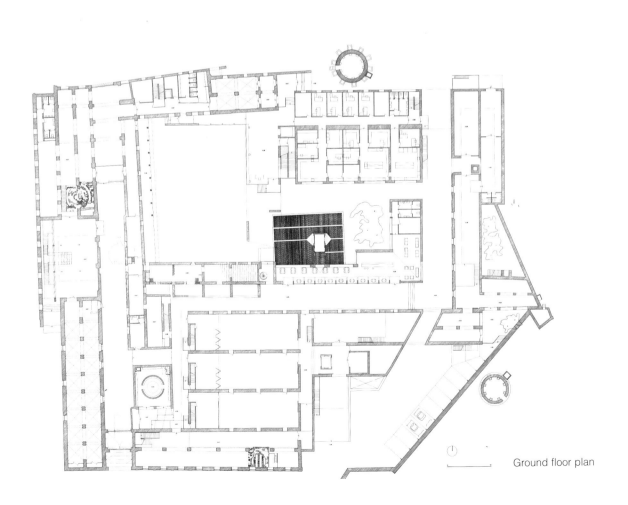
Ground floor plan

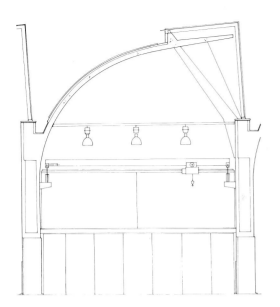

Cross section

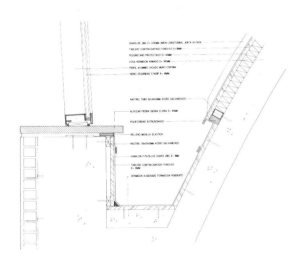

Detail of the roof

Longitudinal section

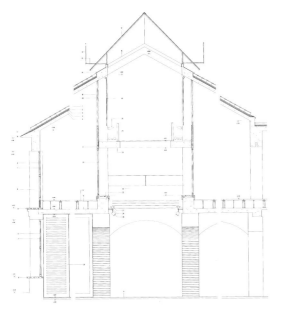

The skylight runs the length of the double-height building that houses the exhibition areas, which stand above the conserved remains of the old warehouses.

Section through administration area

Longitudinal section

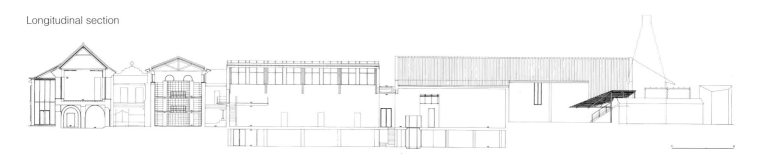

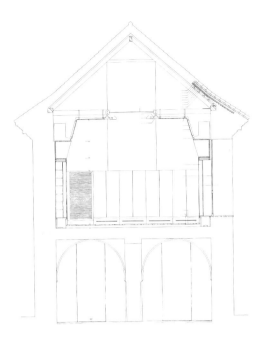

Section through the library

The top floor of the volume standing on the west side houses the reading room of the library. The ceiling is lined with boards made of compressed wood shavings.

117

Eduardo Souto de Moura

& Humberto Vieira

Pousada Santa Maria do Bouro

Amares Portugal

Photographs: Duccio Malagamba

This project aims to adapt, or rather, to make use of stones available to built a new building. It is a new building, in which various voices and functions -some already registered, other still to be constructed- intervene; it is not reconstruction of the building in its original form. For this project, the ruins are more important than the Convent.

It is they that are open and manipulable, just as the building was during its history. This attitude is not meant to express or represent an exceptional case justifying some original manifesto, but rather to abide by a rule of architecture, more or less unchanging throught time. During the design process, a lucidity was sought for between the form and the program. Faced with two possible paths, we chose to reject the pure and simple consolidation of the ruin for the sake of contemplation, opting instead for the introduction of new materials, uses, forms and functions entre les choses, as Corbusier said. The pinturesque is a question of fate, nor part of a projection or program.

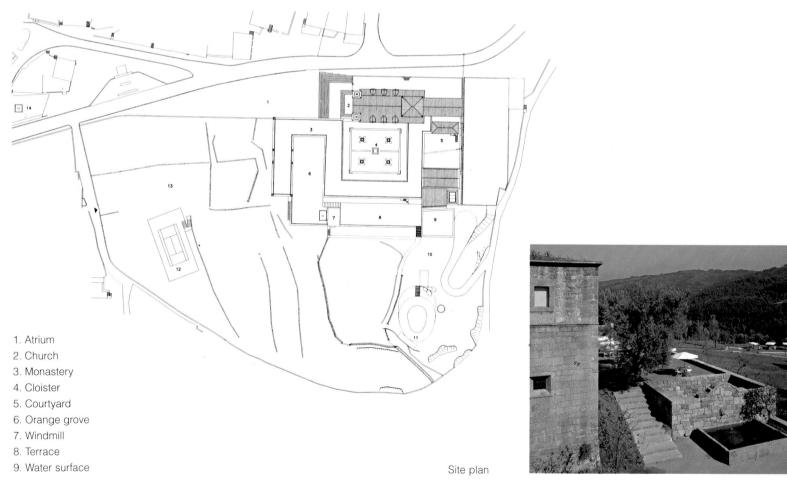

1. Atrium
2. Church
3. Monastery
4. Cloister
5. Courtyard
6. Orange grove
7. Windmill
8. Terrace
9. Water surface

Site plan

The most important value of this project was the meticulous work carried out over several years by Souto de Moura, in which he studied and reinterpreted the ruins of the old monastery to transform it into a *Pousada*. The south facade, with the garden and the pool, a long volume that houses the bedrooms of the hotel staff, and the east wing of this facade in which the restaurant is inserted are the newest elements of the restoration, that was recreated under the suggestions given by the shapes of the ruins themselves.

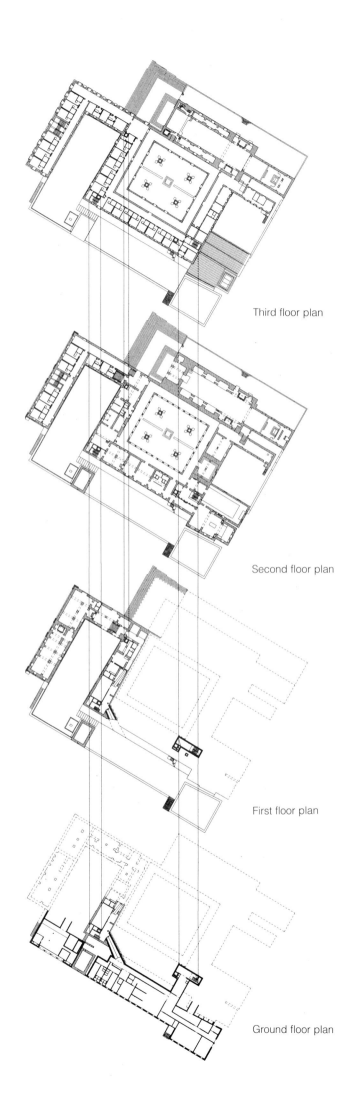

Third floor plan

Second floor plan

First floor plan

Ground floor plan

122

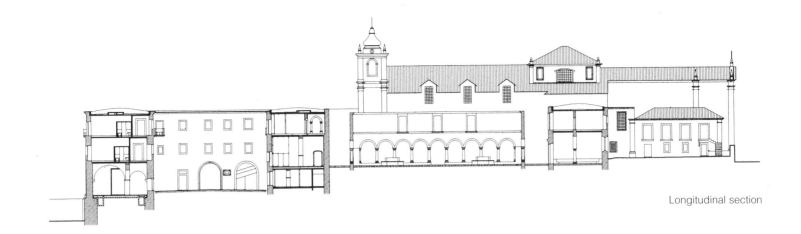

Longitudinal section

123

Inside the building, the space was organized so as to make it as transparent and manipulable as possible. The architect thus brings ample lighting to all corners of the old convent.

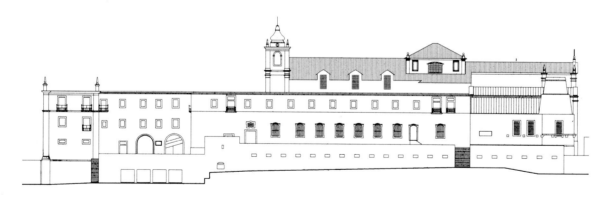

South elevation

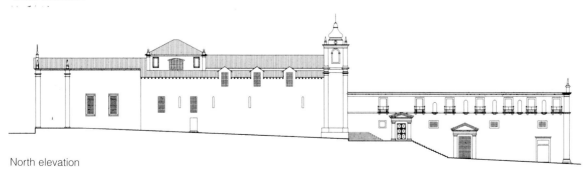

North elevation

One of the essential premises when furnishing the rooms was to maintain the simplicity and the purity of forms that characterizes the historical complex.

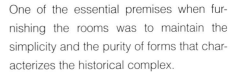

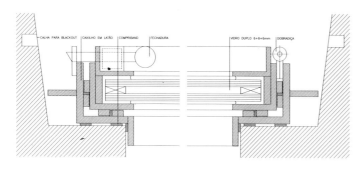

Longitudinal section

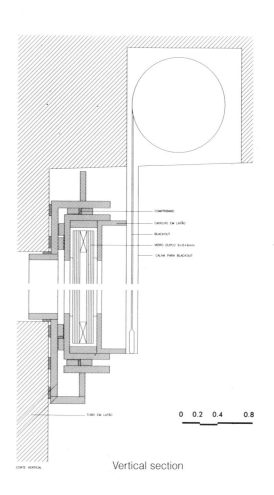

Vertical section

126

Both in the design of the new spaces and in the consolidation of the existing ones, one of the most prominen aspects is the introduction of new materials and forms that do not belong to the original structure of the building.

Claudio Silvestrin

Photographs: Angelo Kaunat

The Johan Restaurant

Graz Austria

The restaurant takes place inside a former 16th century horses stable of 250m² located in centre Graz, in Austria. The British architect Claudio Silvestrin has transformed the historic space into a restaurant of international cuisine.

The original space and architectural features –stone columns and vaulted ceiling– have been restored and preserved, with a respectful spirit.

The careful project conceales heating and cooling installations under the floor and in the wall thickness functioning through new high level windows and niches.

On the other hand, the sandy color of the stone floor has been matched on the walls and ceiling with pigmented plaster and limewash, resulting a serene and warm atmosphere for the whole interior.

Regarding the furniture design, the long bar top, the benches and the Fronzoni tables have been built with the same teak wood. Claudio Silvestrin benches have a high back to suggest solemnity. The dining chairs are upholstered in white canvas, as are the bar stools.

On the other hand, the kitchen is concealed by a 6 foot wall to allow the space of the vaulted ceiling to stretch to its maximum.

As usual in the poetic and serene works by Claudio Silvestrin, he declares that he has intended to be in this new work:

Elegant but not ostentatious.
Simple yet vigorous.
Stunning but not intimidating.
Comfortable but with dignity.
Intimate but not secluded.
Modern yet classical.
Non traditional yet preserving
its origins.
With natural materials only.
Without any black or white.

The project maintains the original structure of the building intact, limiting the height of the new outer walls and allowing the full expression of the arched roof.

1. Entrance hall
2. Cloakroom
3. Toilets
4. Plant room
5. Bar
6. Restaurant
7. Kitchen

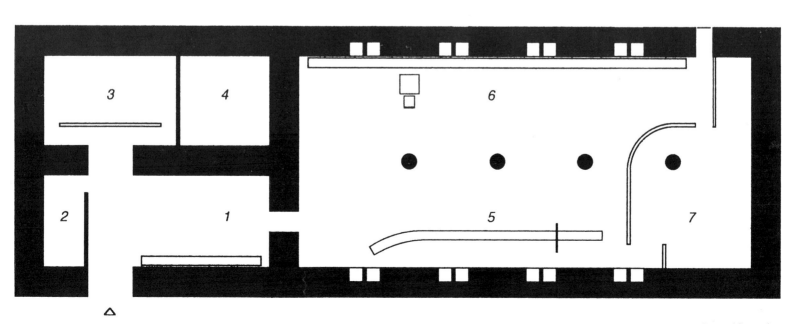

Ground floor plan

The sandy color of the stone floor has been matched on the walls and ceiling with pigmented plaster and limewash, resulting a serene and warm atmosphere in the whole interior.

The subtle architectural project conserves and enhances the atmosphere and architectural characteristics of the old stable in which the restaurant is located.

133

The teak wood used to make the furniture provides the restaurant with a warm skin that contrasts with the neutral walls and roofs. Part of the pieces –the dining chairs and stools– are upholstered in white canvas jackets.

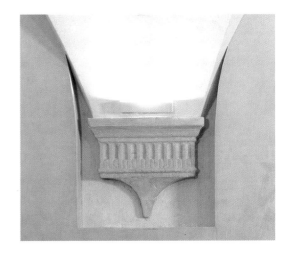

Marc van Schuylenbergh

Photographs: Jan Caudron-Anakasis

Conversion of van Schuylenbergh house

AalstBelgium

Located in a busy street in the Belgian town of Aalst, the architect Van Schuylenberg transformed a century-old worker's dwelling into his own home.

In addition to cleaning the facades and opening new windows in the old building, the architect raised a new, long narrow volume that is attached to the old one through an intermediate space in the form of a wedge that follows the curve of the site. This intermediate area is an area of transit in the interior that is well lit from above. The division between the old wing and the new wing is shown by means of a low curving wall.

In the old volume the pure language of the modern intervention is combined with respect for the singularity of some existing elements, such as floor tiles, window frames, fragments of rustic wall face and the old staircase.

The distribution of the rooms has hardly been changed: there are two bedrooms, one situated behind the other, a narrow hall and a staircase.

Another of the most important elements of the new scheme is a raised walkway that communicates the main bedroom with its bathroom, both of which are located on the first floor over each of the two volumes of the dwelling.

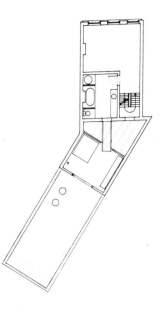

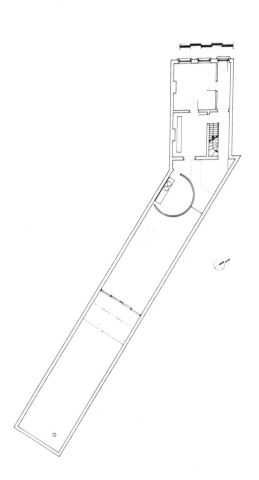

The facade has been modified with new openings that provide better lighting for the interior.

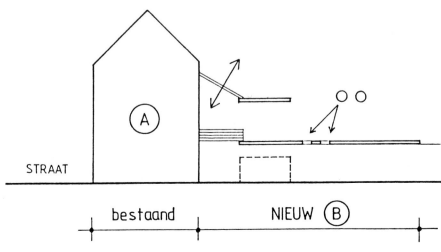

STRAAT

(A)

bestaand | NIEUW (B)

A semicircular wall absorbs the rotation of the site and leads to the living room located at the rear.

Cross section

In the interior, original elements coexist in harmony with the new intervention.

The floors, the doorframes and the old staircase to the upper floor have been conserved.

Massimo & Grabiella Carmassi

Photographs: Mario Ciampi

Two apartments *in* Pisa

Pisa Italy

The clients wanted to make two homes for their sons out of a large apartment located on the top floors of a Renaissance building in via S. Maria, which leads from the Arno to the cathedral. Unfortunately, the apartment had been altered at the beginning of this century, and had lost most of its original features. The structures, floor slabs and original spaces were carefully restored, whilst uncovering nineteenth-century decorations.

The larger flat is formed by a sequence of rooms overlooking the central cloister of the building. To free all the rooms whilst preserving the original type of structure, a long C-shaped passage was created tangent to the cloister, formed in part by an existing corridor. The different insulation requirements of the various spaces were satisfied by differentiating the technological features of door and window frames. Whilst the space adjoining the kitchen consists of a broken partition of transparent glass with an iron frame, that next to the bedrooms is distinguished by cupboards with large cypress doors and a slightly curved section. The demolition of the entrance corridor floor slab made it possible to create a volume two storeys high. This is overlooked by the large living room and dining room and, on the second level, across a light iron walkway, by the terrace and studio.

The smaller and simpler of the two flats comprises a linear sequence of four rooms. Of varying sizes, these have been conserved and restored according to their original styles, and connected by the old two-leaf wooden doors. A Renaissance-style staircase, built in the 1930s, goes up from the living room to the attic. This consists of three rooms looking onto a very small cloister and a double volume, containing the kitchen and part of the stairs. The complex spatial system comprising the little cloister and the double volume is created through a combination of iron and glass partitions and the bearing wall layout. A skylight illuminates this part of the apartment.

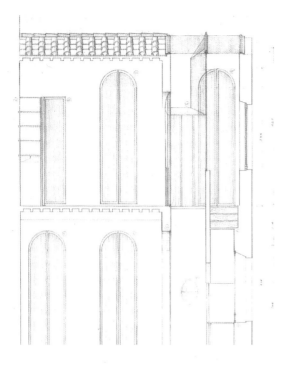

Section AA'

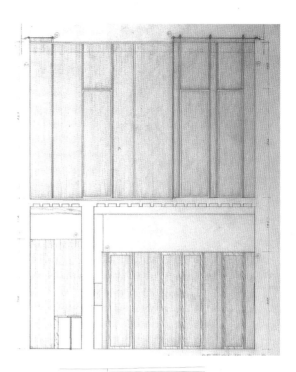

Section BB'

Ground floor plan

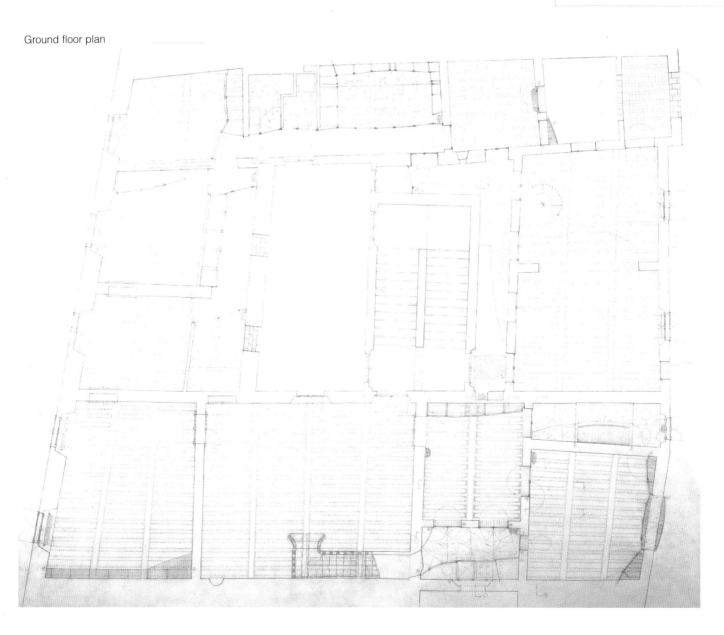

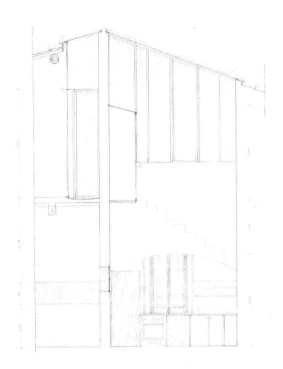

Section CC'

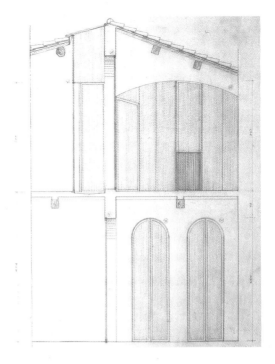

Section DD'

Upper floor plan

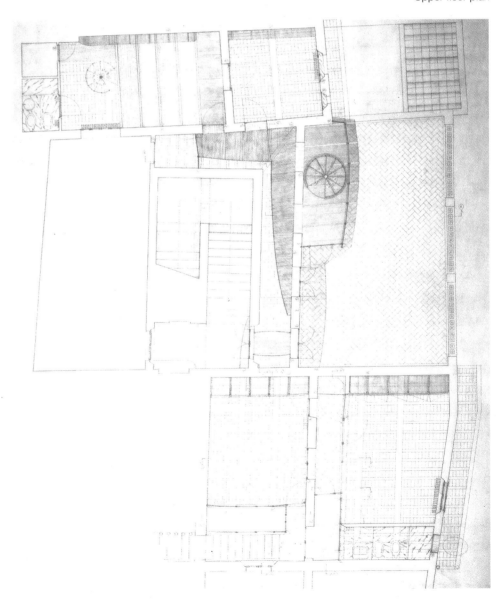

Apartment A

Construction detail of the spiral staircase

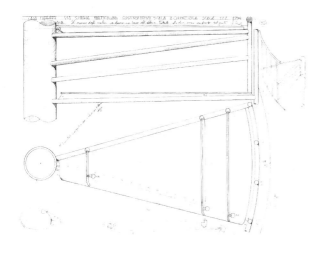

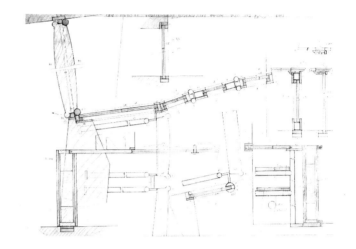

Construction detail

A transparent glass wall separates the kitchen from the corridor. The kitchen cupboards are made of etched glass on a steel structure.

Construction detail of the outer wall of the terrace

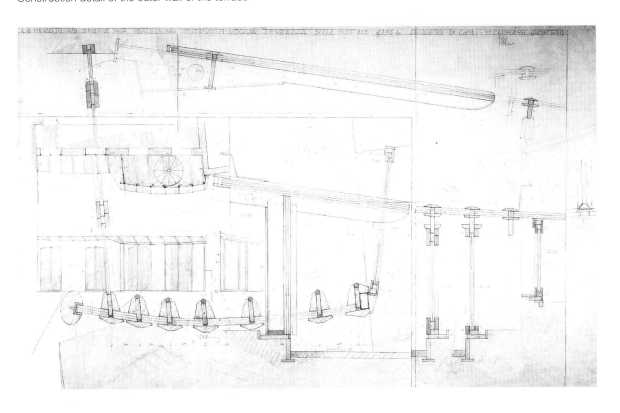

Apartment B

A skylight illuminates the part of the dwelling with few openings, thus allowing light to reach the lower floor.

Axonometric projection

On this page, views of the living room and the bathroom of apartment B.

Derek Wylie Architecture

Lee House

Photographs: Nick Kane

Clerkenwell United Kingdom

In this block in Clerkenwell, a fashionable district of London, the architect has acquired a complex composed of a Victorian building with a shop on the ground floor and a workshop at the end of the court in order to work and live there with his family.

Surrounded by buildings, the narrow and deep plot was graced with little light and even fewer outside views. The project consisted therefore in conceiving fluid spaces in the existing structure and optimising the entrance of natural light by creating an interior court framed by the L-shaped ground plan. To take full advantage of this quiet space, floor-to-ceiling sliding glass panels are used and the court becomes the natural exterior elongation of the living room, whose furniture is equipped with rollers for a highly flexible layout.

Light penetrates the heart of the dwelling through skylights with a wood-covered steel structure that have been created above the kitchen and the mezzanine. Furthermore, the set-back alignment of the facade defined a space of transition between the street and the office, and authorised the use of glass paving that provides direct lighting for the bathroom situated in the basement. In several forms glass facilitates the circuit of light from skylights toward the

inside of the house. In the mezzanine covered with a glass roof, the floor is made of strips of glass and oak that constitute a semi-translucent floor. Outside, the small balcony also has a glass floor in order to avoid casting too much shade on the facade and the court.

This attention to the trajectory of light is found even in the kitchen elements clad in aluminium, of which the high cupboard doors are profiled in order to allow the light to slip from the glass roof toward the working area.

The materials used respond to criteria of simplicity and hardiness. An oak parquet laid on the whole ground floor including the staircase of the entrance accentuates the spatial continuity of this level, with the exception of a part of the kitchen in which the limestone paving of the court continues along the working plane. Drawn in the detail, the two new staircases with oak-clad steps are supported by a steel structure of welded plates for the staircase of the mezzanine, and a tapered mast for the staircase at the rear.

Derek Wylie's project is sober and functional; the existing brick walls have been conserved as they were or just painted blank, a testimony to the history of places that is pursued by the architect.

Site plan

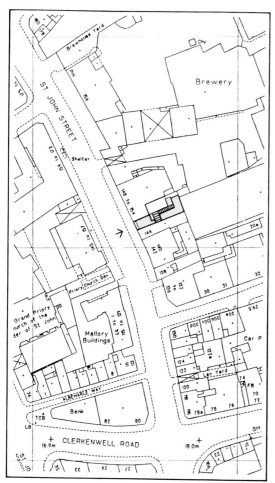

The floor of the hall was made with circular glass blocks set in concrete modules.

All the glass surfaces are translucent to ensure privacy, except for those of the dining room that give views onto the nearby dome.

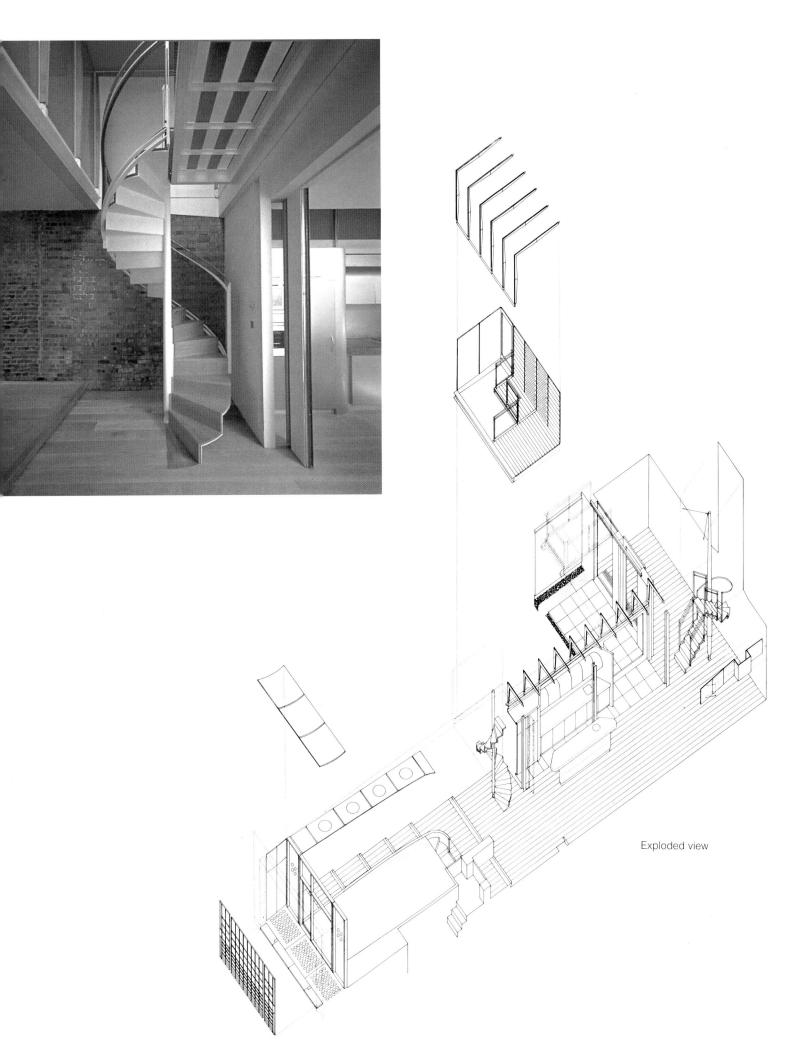

Exploded view

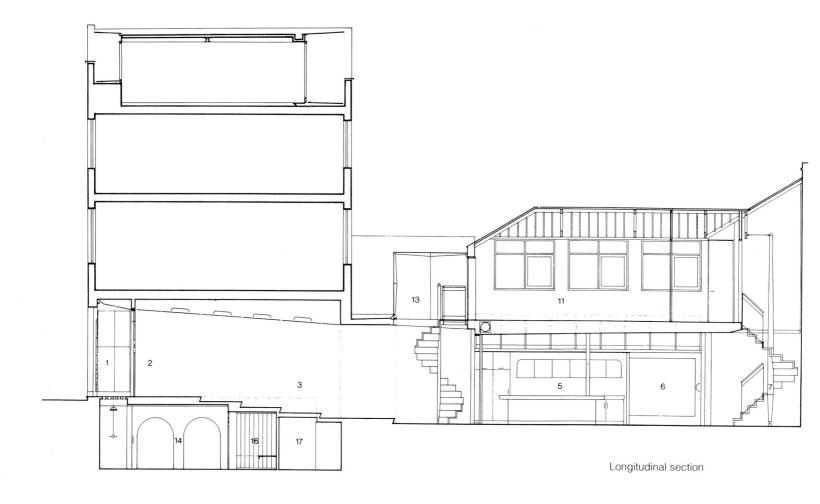

Longitudinal section

1.street lobby 2.house entrance 3.stepped ramp 4.office 5.kitchen 6.dining 7.tv den 8.living 9.courtyard 10.pool 11.bedroom 12.balcony 13.void 14.bathroom 15.mez-
zanine 16.sauna room 17.utility 18.adjoining roof 19.apartment entrance

After Wylie's work, the resulting space exposes the structure of the original buildings, allowing the light and the space to flow freely between the different areas of the dwelling.

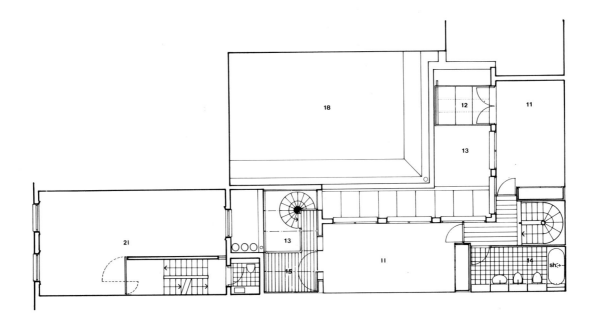

First floor plan

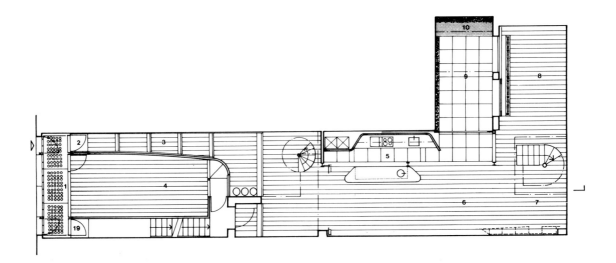

Ground floor plan

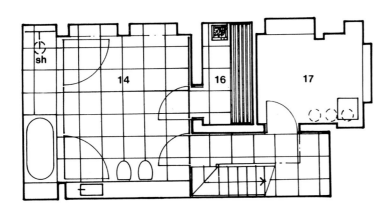

Basement floor plan

In order to maximise the entry of natural light in all the rooms of the studio and the house, an inner courtyard L-shaped was created and becomes the focus of the structure. To take full advantage of this quiet space, floor-to-ceiling sliding glass panels are used and the court becomes the natural exterior elongation of the living room, whose furniture is equipped with rollers for a highly flexible layout.

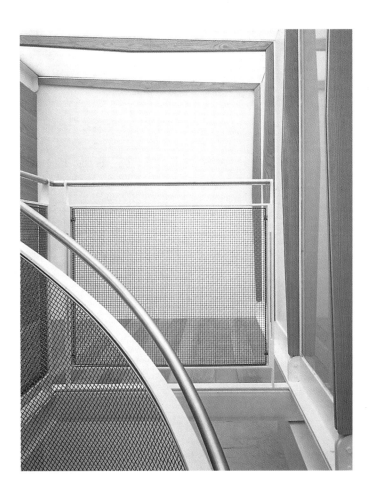

The photographs above this caption show some views of the staircases, and it shows how the alternate use of oak and translucent glass panels in the floor of the mezzanine enhances the sensation of light on the lower floors. To the left, a detailed view of the courtyard balcony.

To the left and below to this caption, one of the bathrooms, where outstands the yellow-painted wall behind the washbasin, that hide several niches for storage, as it is shown on the pictures. A large mirror covers the wall to the right, amplifying the spatial sensation.

Below, a view of the basement bathroom and sauna. Here, the new materials are combined with ones that belong to the old building, as a testimony to the history that is pursued by Wylie in his whole work.

Alexander Runser Christa Prantl

Photographs: Margherita Spiluttini

Lanzendorfer Mühle

MistelbachAustria

In this low-budget conversion of a baroque mill located in a small village some 50 km from Vienna, the brief was to establish a large living area on the roof floor of the old storage building and to create space for a doctor's surgery on the main level; the main level of the residential building was to be remodelled to house the private rooms and a small apartment.

The baroque facade was renovated and the partly destroyed walls protecting the gardens east and west of the building were re-erected. The facade of the cellar level on the east side was excavated and found to be an arcade. It is now the entrance to the doctor's surgery. On the west side of the building a new entrance to the living area was made, which gives access to a staircase going up to the new living area in the roof space.

The main intervention is the installation of a new concrete object at the intersection of the storage building and the long residential building. It is formed as an independent three-dimensional structure with a staircase. Four walls like

plates of bare reinforced concrete define the way into the building. Together with the stairs they define the centre of the house. They create a link between the entrance, the private rooms, the new living space on the roof floor and the surgery in the former storage building. This modern element connects, divides and opens without destroying the antique substance.

Two 20 sqm glass windows in the roof let the light into the entrance hall, the large living space on the roof floor and the rooms of the surgery. Eight glass doors with soundproof glass separate the surgery from the living space. This, and the soundproof construction of the ceiling avoid problems between living and working space of the doctor's family. The object of bare concrete helps the optical separation between living and working area. The mass of this material serves for heat storage, which is necessary for a well-balanced room climate. There was no need for sun protection for the space under the glass roof.

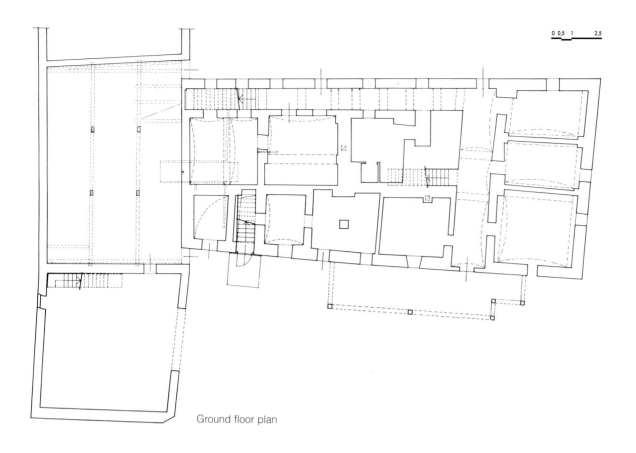

Ground floor plan

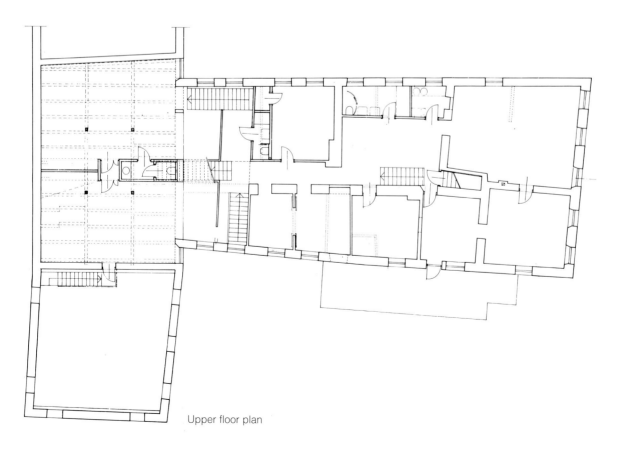

Upper floor plan

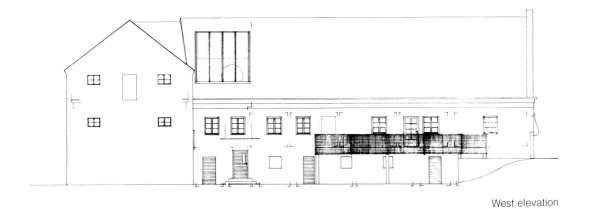

West elevation

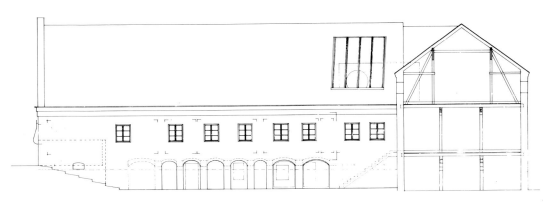

East elevation

Cross section

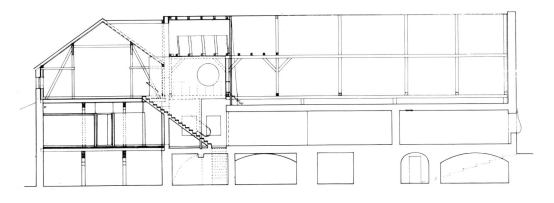

The living area situated under the roof receives plenty of natural light through the two large skylights.

The magnificent assembled wooden structure that supports the sloping roof has been fully restored. The contrast of the varnished wood with the white walls highlights its beauty.

The top photograph shows how the distribution area situated on the ground floor conserves its original structure.
On the right, the reinforced concrete walls define the circulation inside the building.

Two different views of the waiting room of the new working area. It is located in an area that was originally used for storage.

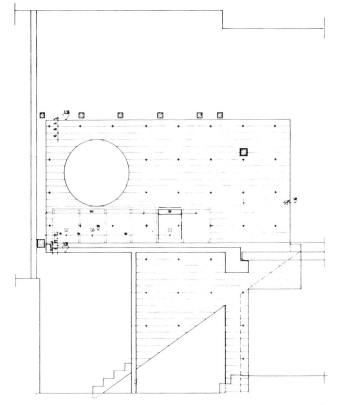

0 0,5 1   2

Longitudinal section

The intersection of the storage building and the long residential building was solved using a three-dimensional structure formed by four reinforced concrete walls.

The central element formed by the four concrete walls connects, divides and opens the space without destroying the essence of the building and gives a certain air of renewed modernity.

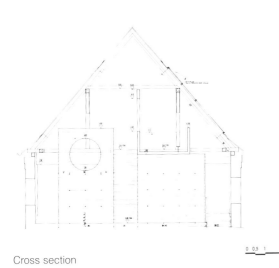

Cross section

Seth Stein

Photographs: Richard Bryant / ARCAID

House *in* Kensington

London United Kingdom

This house, where the British architect Seth Stein lives with his family, is a former builder's yard located in Kensington, a residential London district.

The house is a highly personal interpretation of the typical Victorian terraced houses of the district, although the found structure –a stableyard, built in the 1880s– has been retrained and a wide variety of architectural (Roman atrium house, traditional Japanese garden) and pictorial (Matisse fucsia) references have been added. In fact, Stein has created an atrium house in the proper Roman sense, in spirirt but not in execution akin to the sequestered houses of more southerly latitudes.

The design exploits the long narrow plot that was once also a construction yard with an entrance block set back from the street to create a "public" forecourt to offset private patio court around which the uninterupted sequence of space extends like an architectural promenade of unusual rigour and simplicity.

When acquired by the Steins, the site was open on the south side to the street, at the rear were remnants of Victorian stables in a state of extreme delapidation, while the western edge was lined by an old factory. The house revolves around a long rectangular courtyard, extending at the front and rear over two levels. The introspection has the curious effect of distancing the house from its closest monolithic neighbour, the flats next door.

The extent of the building is large –325 sq m below, 140 sq m above– but the house sits lightly on the site, the scale is domestic and there is the usual domestic arrangement whereby the ground floor is given over to living space, and the upper to sleeping. On the west, the ground floor of the factory is one large kitchen/family room looking on to the garden, its linearity accentuated by the extraordinarily long kitchen counter.

At the back, the Victorian remnants have provided supporting beams and columns on the ground floor; at the upper level the original brick shell with the old windows and exposed trusses has been restored and encloses the bedroom.

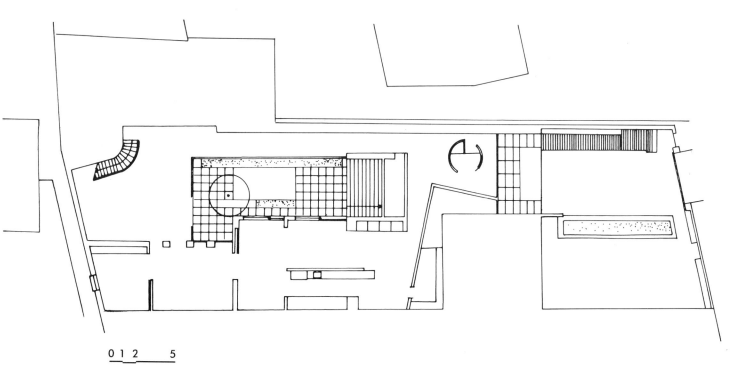

0 1 2   5

Ground floor plan

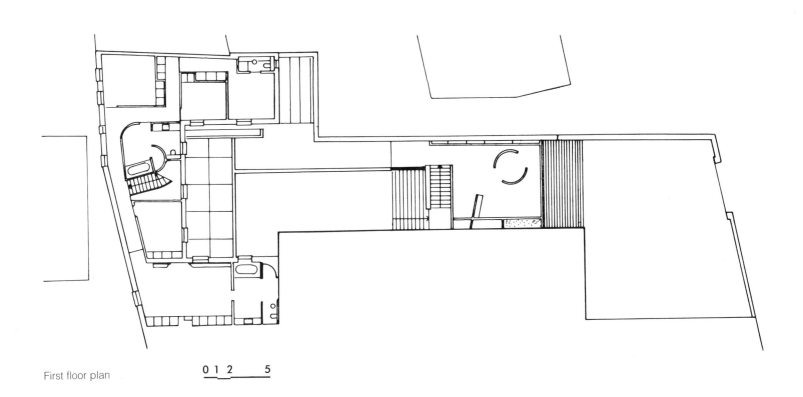

First floor plan

0 1 2   5

On the ground floor and located near the entrance hall there is a small cylindrical volume of concrete whose silhouette stands out against a fucsia coloured wall. This wall has been designed to contain a toilet and it rises in the exterior through the roof terrace.

The living room is furnished with sofas, that can be seen on the righ, recently created by the British designer Marc Newson, and that are upholstered in fabric of bright colours.

182